Catholics Don't Read the Bible— Who Says?

Rebecca Hinton

ISBN 979-8-89345-907-4 (paperback)
ISBN 979-8-89345-906-7 (digital)

Christian Faith Publishing
832 Park Avenue
Meadville, PA 16335
www.christianfaithpublishing.com

Printed in the United States of America

> As I poured out my heart to the Lord [fol-lowing the loss of a baby]…[H]e brought to mind Scriptures I had memorized long ago from Hebrews 11 and 12. (Please note how important it was that I had memorized these Scriptures so that God could bring them to my heart in a time of crisis when I had no access to [H]is Word. Catholics can and must memorize Scripture—Protestants have no special gene that makes it easier for them to do it). (147)

Thus states Kimberly Hahn, a Catholic convert and former Presbyterian. While Hahn intends only to stress the power of Scripture in a time of trial, her assumption that Catholics do not learn biblical verses by heart brings to mind a related and fairly wide-spread misunderstanding among non-Catholics: namely, that despite their piety, many Catholics neither know nor read the Bible at all, let alone use it as a guide and solace. Nothing could be more contrary to the truth!

Growing up, I regarded Bible reading as a "Protestant thing," probably because I witnessed few Catholics reading or discussing Scripture. Instead, we attended Mass, prayed the Rosary, venerated saints. Although we acknowledged Holy Scripture as the Word of God, most of us failed to memorize or meditate on its contents to the extent that Protestants did. Over the years, however, my fellow Catholics seem to have taken a greater interest in the Bible. Pastors frequently base their sermons on scriptural passages, and many parishes now offer Bible classes for both children and adults.

Catholics may have based their hesitation to read the Bible on a mandate from the Council of Trent (Fourth Session, "Decree Concerning the Edition and Use of the Sacred Books"), which forbids individual, or private, interpretation of Scripture. This mandate acts as a safeguard, for readers acting solely on their own understanding of given passages (often removed from their contexts) have used the Bible to justify everything from genocide to polygamy. The rule against private interpretation notwithstanding, however, the Church has always encouraged Her members, both clerical and lay, to embrace Sacred Scripture and apply it to their lives.

Therefore, the following material does not intend to teach well-informed, practicing Catholics what they already know. (This would be preaching to the choir.) Neither does it purport to cover every reference to Scripture in the Church's liturgy. Rather, it presents examples to show well-meaning but misinformed non-Catholics that despite stereotypes depicting Catholics as having gotten away from the true biblical spirit of Christianity, the Church abounds in Scripture, in both her public liturgy and the private lives of her people.

The Mass Itself Includes a Big Chunk of the Bible

Some years ago, I had taken my missal to work so that on breaks, I could read over the propers for the coming Sunday. A friend and colleague, a devout Baptist, noticed the missal's black cover and mistook it for a Bible. "You're reading the Bible!" she exclaimed in amazement. I explained that while the missal was a Mass book, it did contain a big chunk of the Bible. Indeed, by taking a look at the individual prayers in the traditional Tridentine Mass, we can see that roughly 70 percent of them appear in Scripture.

The Mass propers are rich in passages from the Old and New Testaments. While the proper Gospel and lesson echo the messages of Christ and Saint Paul, respectively (although the lesson sometimes replaces Saint Paul's letter to the early Christians with verses from the Apocalypse or a reading from the Old Testament), the Introit, the Gradual, the Offertory, and the Communion usually incorporate the words of a Psalm.

Similarly, the prayers of the Ordinary ring with the words of Scripture. "Judica me, Deus (Judge me, God)…," the first prayer at the foot of the altar, is Psalm 42; while "Deus, tu conversus (Having turned, O God)…" contains the words of Psalm 125. The oft-repeated phrase "Domine, exaudi orationem meam et clamor meus ad te veniat" (O Lord, hear my prayer and let my cry come unto thee) recalls King David's plea in Psalm 102:2, and who can forget the angels' greeting to the shepherds in the opening of the Gloria: "Gloria in excelsis Deo et in terra pax hominibus bonae voluntatis" (Glory to God in the highest and peace to men of good will)?

After reading the Epistle, or Lesson, the celebrant moves to the center of the altar, where he prays the "Munda cor meum" ("Cleanse my heart and my lips, O almighty God, who didst cleanse with a burning coal the lips of the prophet Isaiah"), asking God to let him worthily read the Gospel. This plea comes from the sixth chapter of Isaiah, where one of the seraphim touches the prophet's lips with a burning coal, enabling him to teach and speak to his people with a clean mouth and a clean soul (Isaiah 6:2–7).

Moving from the Mass of the Catechumens (those prayers preceding and including the Credo) to the Offertory, the priest offers the wine with the words "Offerimus tibi, Domine, calicem salutaris, tuam deprecantes clementiam" (We offer to Thee, O Lord, the chalice of salvation, beseeching Thy mercy), praying that the offering may ascend "odore suavitatis" (with an odor of sweetness). The phrase "odore suavitatis" occurs numerous times in Leviticus when Moses gives explicit directions for offering the Hebrew sacrifice (See Leviticus 1:9, 2:2, 2:9, 3:5, 3:16, 6:15, 6:21, 8:12, 8:28, 12:12, 17:6, 23:13). Next, the priest recites the Lavabo (Psalm 25) before moving on to the prayers begging God to accept our sacrifice.

Following the "Suscipe sancta Trinitas" (Receive, Holy Trinity), the "Orate frates" (Pray, Brethren) and the Secret, the priest proceeds to the Canon of the Mass, preceding it by the Preface, which may vary depending on the liturgical day or the occasion of the Mass (e.g., a Mass honoring Our Lady or an Apostle or a Mass for the deceased). The Preface ends again with a slight variation of the words of Isaiah when he relates his vision of the Lord sitting on His throne, surrounded by a throng of angels, who cry, "Sanctus, sanctus, sanctus Dominus exercituum; plena est omnis terra Gloria ejus" (Holy, holy, holy Lord of hosts; all the earth is full of His glory). In addition, the throng of Hebrews shouted these words, strewing Our Lord's path with palm branches, as He rode into Jerusalem.

The essential words of the Canon of the Mass—that is, the words of consecration—come directly from Christ's words at the Last Supper when He changed the bread and wine into His body and blood. Following the Consecration and the prayers to God, the patriarchs, and the saints, priest and people pray the Our Father, the prayer taught by Jesus Himself.

At the Communion, we encounter the words of the centurion in Matthew 8:8, those of King David, and those of John the Baptist. Prior to receiving Communion, the priest repeats the centurion's protest when Our Lord comes to cure his servant: "Domine, non sum dignus ut intres sub tectum meum; sed tantum dic verbo et sanabitur puer meus" (Matthew 8:8) (O Lord, I am not worthy that You should enter under my roof; but only say the word and my servant shall be healed), substituting "anima mea" (my soul) for "puer meus." After receiving the consecrated Host, he asks, as does David in Psalm 115, verse 12, "Quis retribuam Domino pro omnibus quae retribuit mihi?" (What will I give back to the Lord for all that He has given to me?) Finally, before distributing Holy Communion to the faithful, the celebrant elevates the Sacred Host and recites the tidings of John the Baptist when he proclaims Jesus of Nazareth as the long-awaited Messiah: "Ecce Agnus Dei, ecce qui tollit peccata mundi" (Behold the Lamb of God, behold Him Who takes away the sins of the world) (John 1:29). After the Communion of the faithful and the closing prayers, the Mass concludes with the Last Gospel: the first chapter of John, verses 1–14.

The foregoing material applies to any Mass, high or low. A solemn high Mass, on the other hand, begins with the "Asperges me" (Thou wilt sprinkle me …), from Psalm 50:9. During the Paschal season, the "Vidi aquam" (I saw water), based on a vision of Ezekiel, replaces "Asperges me."

These examples represent only a few of the biblical passages in the Tridentine Mass. However, they suffice to show that even if a Catholic never opened a Bible, he or she would still receive a sizable exposure to the Word of God by attentively assisting at the Mass.

Not only the Mass but the entire liturgy is richly scriptural. The Tenebrae services on the evenings of Holy Week, for example, come from the lamentations of the prophets, mainly Jeremiah. Moreover, the Divine Office, which the priests recite, covers all one hundred and fifty Psalms in a given week; and finally, the quintessential Catholic prayer, the Hail Mary, originates from the Gospel of

Saint Luke, when the angel Gabriel greets Mary, saying, "Ave, gratia plena; Dominus tecum" (Hail, full of grace; the Lord [is] with thee) (Luke 1:28) and when Elizabeth hails the Mother of God with the words, "Benedicta tu inter mulieris et benedictus fructus ventris tui" (Blessed art thou among women and blessed is the fruit of thy womb) (Luke 1:42).

Moreover, certain institutions, practices, and beliefs unique to Catholics have their foundations in Scripture. Those accustomed to seeing Protestant ministers wearing a simple, dark robe may be mystified by the ornate, multilayered linen vestments of the Catholic priests, their colors varying with the liturgical seasons and the feast days; but although such vestments may seem needlessly fancy to outsiders, they recall those worn by the ancient Hebrew priests. In Exodus 28, for example, God gives Moses explicit and detailed instructions regarding the garb of the first priests, Aaron and his sons: "And thou shalt speak to all the wise of heart, whom I have filled with the spirit of wisdom, that they may make Aaron's vestments, in which he being consecrated may minister to me. And these shall be the vestments that they shall make: a rational and an ephod, a tunick [sic] and a straight linen garment, a mitre [sic] and a girdle. They shall make the holy vestments for the brother Aaron and his sons, that they may do the office of the priesthood unto me... And they shall make the ephod of gold, and violet, and purple, and scarlet twice dyed, and fine linen. It shall have the two edges joined in the top of both sides, that they may be closed together" (3, 4, 6, 7). Although the vestments of Catholic priests differ from those of the Hebrews, God seems to have made it clear from ancient times that those who offer His sacrifice must dress according to strict specifications.

In addition, the Lord tells Moses the requirements for the altar on which the priests will offer their sacrifices. It must be made of "setim wood" (Exodus 27:1) and must hold a lamp filled with "the purest oil of the olives, beaten with a pestle, that [it] may burn always" (Exodus 27:20), similar to the sanctuary lamp in Catholic churches. As in the case of the vestments, the altar must conform to stringently prescribed characteristics.

Like the members of some ancient religions, present-day Catholics pray for the souls of the dead, believing that even if individuals die in God's grace, lacking mortal sin, most must undergo a state of spiritual cleansing before meeting their divine Maker face-to-face. This state the Church calls Purgatory (from the Latin infinitive *purgare*, meaning "to cleanse." Although the Bible does not contain the word purgatory, it contains the concept: In 2 Maccabees, chapter 12, Judas Maccabeus, having vanquished many enemies of the Jews and buried a great number of his own people, "sent twelve thousand drachmas of silver to Jerusalem for sacrifice to be offered for the sins of the dead, thinking well and religiously concerning the resurrection, ([f]or if he had not hoped that they that were slain should rise again, it would have seemed superfluous and vain to pray for the dead,) and because he considered that they who had fallen asleep with godliness had great grace laid up for them. It is therefore a holy and wholesome thought to pray for the dead, that they may be loosed from sins" (Forrest 43–46). From these verses, it is clear that the ancient Jews, the forerunners of the Christians, believed in an afterlife state in which the dead could atone for any venial, or pardonable, sins still on their souls. Father M. D. Forrest also points out verse 32 in Matthew 12: "And whosoever shall speak a word against the Son of man, it shall be forgiven him: but he that shall speak against the Holy Ghost, it shall not be forgiven in him, neither in this world nor in the world to come." Father explains, "The fact that [Our Lord] spoke of a certain sin not being forgiven 'either in this world or in the world to come' implies… that there are some sins (venial sins) which may be remitted in the world to come, and that there must, therefore, be an intermediate state of purification or expiation [between heaven and hell], which we call purgatory" (185).

But what about the forgiveness of sins committed while one is still on earth? Non-Catholics often ask why Catholics confess their sins to a priest and "ascribe to a mere man a power that belongs to God alone? No one but God can forgive sin" (Forrest 144). Before He ascended, Christ gave His apostles (the first Christian priests) power to act as His agents in forgiving sins. Saint Matthew quotes Him as saying, "Whatsoever you shall bind on earth shall be bound also in heaven; and whatsoever you shall loose on earth shall be loosed also in heaven" (28:18). Again, Our Lord says in the Gospel of Saint John, "Receive ye the Holy Ghost. Whose sins you shall forgive, they are forgiven them; and whose sins you shall retain, they are retained" (20:21–23).

The foregoing examples present only a sampling. Hopefully, however, they will show that far from being a "scriptureless" religion, Catholicism contains many biblical references and rests heavily on the Word of God.

The Church Has Always Encouraged Her Members to Read the Bible

Session 4 of the Council of Trent notwithstanding, the Catholic Church has always upheld Holy Scripture as a source of knowledge and inspiration. Four popes of the late nineteenth and early twentieth centuries have been especially vociferous in their defense of Bible reading. In his 1893 encyclical *Proventissimus Deus*, for instance, Pope Leo XIII (1878–1903) quotes Timothy, a colleague of Saint Paul, who says, "All Scripture inspired by God is profitable to teach, to reprove, to correct, to instruct in justice, that the man of God may be perfect, furnished to every good work" (quoted in article 3, page 5). The pope goes on to say that although there exist "men of talent and learning, who devote themselves with ardor to the defense of sacred writings and to making them known and better understood… we cannot but exhort others… to give themselves to the same praiseworthy work" (article 2, page 5). Since these "others" are presumably laymen, his admonition seems directed not only to clerics and theologians but to all members of the Church. He also recommends that those who are able read the Bible in its original languages (article 17, pages 21–22).

To avoid the danger of private interpretation, however, Leo XIII calls for seminary instructors knowledgeable in Scripture and able to teach future priests to defend the Word of God against skeptics who regard biblical accounts as mere fables and miracles as no more than acts of nature. Such training will enable priests, in turn, to guide their parishioners in doing the same (articles 10–12, pages 12–14). The pope further advises priests and laity to prepare themselves for refuting doubters by learning the principles of natural science and the cultural/historical contexts of biblical events (article 18, page 24).

Reiterating much of his predecessor's advice, Pope Pius X (1903–1914) saw the Bible as a tool for defense and stresses the importance of well-informed teachers of Scripture. A staunch and knowledgeable foe of modernism, a heretical movement that attempted to replace faith and divine revelation with reason alone (Laux 581), he claims in his 1907 encyclical *Praestantia Scripturae* (*The Excellence of Scripture*) that Catholics can use the Bible to disprove modernist errors. Like Leo XIII, he insists that those who teach Scripture in seminaries thoroughly understand the fallacies of heresy and the means to deny them, passing on their knowledge to priests, who will then transmit it to lay the people under their spiritual direction. Only those individuals faithful to the Church's teachings and explicitly opposed to modernism should be permitted to teach. The pope concludes his encyclical with the warning,

> Wherefore we again and most earnestly exhort the ordinaries of the dioceses and the heads of religious congregations to use the utmost vigilance over teachers, and first of all in the seminaries; and should they find any of them imbued with the errors of the modernists and eager for what is new and noxious, or lacking in docility to the prescriptions of the Apostolic See, in whatsoever way published, let them absolutely forbid the teaching office to such; so too, let them exclude from sacred orders those young men who give the faintest reason for doubt that they favor condemned doctrines and pernicious novelties.

Following the example of Leo XIII and Pius X, Pope Benedict XV (1914–22) endorses the use of Scripture among both clergy and laity. Upholding preaching as the most effective means of aiding salvation, he encourages parish priests to deliver frequent sermons based on the Bible, interspersing his encyclical *Humani generis redemptionem* (*For the Redemption of the Human Race: On Preaching the Word of God*) with numerous verses from the letters of Saints Peter and Paul, the Gospels, and the Acts of the Apostles and quoting the words of Saint Mark: "Go ye into the world and preach the Gospel" (16:15). The Gospel, in fact, "is the means Divinely employed to continue the work of eternal salvation" (article 1). Therefore, the Church must take vigilance that both preachers themselves and the messages they preach conform to this end.

Since many priests and lay preachers have incorporated into their sermons an erroneous understanding of Scripture, or use the pulpit as a political platform, he urges bishops to make sure that the priests in their dioceses possess a pure and faultless knowledge of the Bible and pass it on to their listeners (articles 6 and 7). Recalling the fifth session of the Council of Trent, "The Establishment of Lectureships in Holy Scripture and the Liberal Arts," the pope also stresses that preachers of the Word should be academically and morally fit to exercise this ministry.

Finally, in the encyclical *Divino afflante Spiritu*, Pope Pius XII (1939–58) affirms and expands upon the messages of the foregoing popes. During the unstable years between World War I and World War II, he emphasizes the need for lay Catholics to read the Bible and meditate on its contents (8–9), quoting Pius X: "[Bible reading among the laity] is a most useful undertaking [and a means] to dissipate the idea that the Church is opposed to or in any way impedes the reading of the Scripture in the vernacular" (quoted in DAS 8). Nevertheless, like Leo XIII, Pius XII encourages readers and biblical exegetes to peruse the books of the Bible in their original languages, if possible (11–12), and to acquire a fundamental knowledge of natural science. He also encourages familiarity with the historical contexts of the New Testament books (and presumably those of the Old Testament) as well as the contexts of other works written during these times. Such knowledge will help readers to comprehend seemingly strange references and concepts.

Moreover, this pontiff endorsed Bible reading not only for adults but also for children and families. Alden Hatch and Seamus Walsh report that "In a letter written for a new Catholic family Bible, Pius demolished the old canard that the Church discourages her children from reading the Scriptures" (242). In the pope's own words, "The pious reading of the Sacred Scriptures, which the Catholic Church has ever proposed to her faithful children for their sanctification and instruction, is a most fruitful source of spiritual blessings upon the home, serving as an antidote to the undermining influences that threaten on all sides the sacred citadel of the Christian family in the modern world" (quoted in Hatch and Walsh 242).

Nonetheless, Pius XII agrees with his predecessors that correct understanding of the Bible begins with well-informed seminary instructors. He insisted on instructors' having licensure to teach as well as a formal background in Scripture, thus continuing the innovations of Pius X, who established the licentiate and doctorate in scriptural studies in addition to a prescribed method of teaching Scripture in seminaries (7). By setting up and maintaining a tightly defined program of scriptural study at the roots (i.e., in the seminaries), both popes seem to have ensured correct understanding of the Bible and guarded against private interpretation.

The crux of the foregoing encyclicals seems to be not only the importance of scriptural reading but the formal qualifications of those leading or teaching it. While lay Catholics should certainly read the Bible, they should do so with the guidance of the Church's magisterium.

These popes, however, were not the first Church officials to endorse Bible reading. From the earliest days of Christianity, the Church has emphasized the importance of the Bible for both clerics and laity. As the Reverend Henry G. Graham states, during the Middle Ages, bishops required the priests in their dioceses to thoroughly know and comprehend the Bible and in some cases, to memorize it in whole or in part (50). The priests, in turn, incorporated Scripture into their sermons; every church owned at least one full Bible (46), and pastors attached a copy to a stone so that laypeople might read and study it for themselves (53). Even those Christians unable to read learned the Word of God not only through sermons but also through such media as statues, pictures, and plays (53). Thus, since the beginning of the faith, Christians had abundant exposure to and knowledge of Scripture.

While numerous examples can illustrate the above information, let me present a few excerpts from the correspondence of Saint Jerome, one of my favorite Church Fathers. A brilliant scholar, linguist, and prolific writer best known for his translation of Scripture into Latin (the common reading language throughout the Roman Empire), Saint Jerome (c. 347–420) also wrote interpretive theses as well as many letters to friends and colleagues containing discussions of the Bible. Like his successors, the aforementioned popes, Jerome stressed not only the importance of Bible reading itself but also of men equipped to teach Scripture to clergy and laity. Since his primary audience consisted of patrician Romans, we can assume that the readers owned a Bible and were literate in Latin as well as in Hebrew and Greek, the original languages of the Old and New Testament, respectively. In a letter to a priest named Paulinus, for example, Jerome refers to Saint Paul, who "ad pedes Gamaliel legem et prophetas didicisse se gloriatur" (he glories that he learned the law and the prophets at the feet of [the teacher] Gamaliel). Thanks to Gamaliel's instruction, he is armed with "spiritalibus telis" (spiritual darts), which enable him to speak confidently. In turn, Saint Paul instructed the future priest Timothy in Sacred Scripture and advised the bishop Titus to include in his sermons material from the Bible (letter 53, pages 446–447).

Similarly, he urges Pammachius, a young man about to become a cleric or a monk, to frequently read the Bible and keep it always at hand, so that, like Saint Paul, he can "exhortari in doctrina sana et contradicentes revincere" (exhort in sane teaching and refute contradictions) (letter 52, paragraph 7).

Jerome corresponded not only with men but also with women, especially Christian ladies of upper-class Rome. Literate and learned, these women took a lively interest in the Bible and often asked the saint for his understanding of particular books and passages. (See comment about illiterate, page 452, letter 53). As well as expanding his readers' knowledge of Scripture, Jerome encourages his readers to regard Holy Writ as a source of inspiration, hope, and love. Such a reader is Laeta, a young Roman matron who has recently given birth to Paula, a long-awaited child. Because Laeta has consecrated her daughter to God even before conception, Jerome likens her to Anna, the mother of Samuel, who promised to give her yet-to-be-conceived child to the temple (1 Kings 1). As God rewarded Anna by giving her five more children, the saint feels confident that Laeta will reap a similar blessing: "Fiden loquor accepturam te filios quae primum foetum domino reddisti" (I speak with confidence that you, who have rendered your first child to the Lord, will receive children) (letter 107, paragraph 3, page 305).

In addition to commending Laeta's decision to consecrate Paula, Jerome exhorts his friend, apparently a recent convert to Christianity, not to despair concerning her father's paganism. He urges her to persevere in prayer and reminds her of the thief who hung beside Christ on Calvary. Despite his past sins, the thief confessed at the last minute and went to paradise (paragraph 1, page 290). At no time does Saint Jerome seem to question Laeta's familiarity with either of these biblical accounts. On the contrary, he appears to assume that the Bible forms part of her everyday reading.

Saint Jerome hopes that when Paula becomes older and learns to read, she will love the Word of God and use it as a guide. The proverbs of Solomon, for example, will teach her life skills ("ad vitam") while Ecclesiasticus will accustom her to spurn worldly enticements; from the book of Job she will acquire strength and patience, while the Psalms and the Song of Songs will delight her with their poetry (paragraph 12, pages 302–303). Like her mother, Paula will grow up with the Bible as part of her life.

As he advises Laeta to regard Scripture as a source of hope, Jerome offers similar advice to the Virgins of Haemonenses, apparently a group of consecrated ladies living in an ancient community who have become remiss in following their calling. Although he upbraids their laxity, the saint admonishes the women to take heart from the parable of the prodigal son and from the example of the repentant thief on Calvary. The Lord Himself accepted these reprobates, never withholding their love. As in his correspondence with

Laeta, Saint Jerome seems sure of his readers' acquaintance with these stories (letter 11).

Despite his reputation as a misogynist, Jerome praised intelligence and mental curiosity in women. As mentioned above, his circle of friends included members of the female sex. In discussing Scripture with women, he not only recommended the Bible as a means of personal strength but also welcomed perceptive inquiries. His most ardent followers, in fact, seem to have been a group of Roman virgins and matrons who sought his exegeses regarding specific parts of the Old and New Testaments.

Priscilla, a young woman and a consecrated virgin, belonged to this group. Responding to her questions about several obscurities in Psalm 44, he replies that some of the words lost their original meanings when translated from Hebrew to Latin and explains the names of particular persons (letter 65). Although Priscilla is not a cleric but a laywoman, Jerome not only commends her reading of the Bible but also encourages her scrutiny concerning its contents.

While Priscilla seems to have focused mostly on material in the Old Testament, Marcella, a Roman matron, presented five distinct questions in the New: How are we to know God? Who are the sheep and the goats? What is the significance of the Lord's coming in a cloud? How did Christ speak to Mary Magdalene after His resurrection and who was present at His ascension? Saint Jerome answers each question in depth, to the best of his keen understanding. Furthermore, he seems to welcome Marcella's queries as a remedy for his own mental sluggishness, for he writes in the beginning of the letter, "Magnis [me] provocas questionibus et torpens otio ingenium, dum interrogas, doces" (You challenge me with great questions and my mind [which has become] lazy through leisure; while you ask, you teach) (letter 59).

In another letter to Marcella, Saint Jerome replies to her questions regarding the names which the ancient Hebrews used to designate God. She has asked him to list the names and explain the Hebrew meaning of each. Jerome's phrase "studiossime postulasti" (You have asked very studiously) implies that he respects and commends Marcella's intellectual curiosity (letter 25).

From the foregoing examples, we can see that Saint Jerome wanted his correspondents, both male and female, to read, probe, and question Holy Scripture. At the same time, however, he acknowledges the need to do so under the guidance of trained instructors, such as priests with a strong background in scriptural study, lest a lay reader's private interpretation lead him or her astray. As a priest and bishop himself, Jerome seems willing and eager to assume this role.

Moving ahead to the late sixth or early seventh centuries, Pope Gregory I, also known as Pope Gregory the Great (590–604), offers solid advice in *Pastoral Care* (*Regula pastoralis*), a treatise he composed for the guidance of parish priests and the bishops overseeing their work. Although the pope seems in favor of lay Christians' knowing the Word of God, he warns those preaching to them against two potential dangers: a false understanding and interpretation of Scripture (through either ignorance or heresy) and knowledge of the Bible as a means of pride. Erroneous comprehension obviously leads to misunderstanding among the laity and deliberate distortion of biblical passages (i.e., heresy) "slay[s] the minds of the faithful who have already conceived some measure of the understanding of truth" (173). Like Saint Jerome, Pope Gregory stresses the importance of knowledgeable and suitable teachers.

Finally, Saint Bernard, a twelfth-century abbot of Clairvaux, known as the Mellifluous Doctor because of the eloquence of his diction, influenced his monks and others through sermons and letters interspersed with numerous references to the Bible. Although he addressed the majority of his writings to his monastic brothers and clerical acquaintances, the saint also composed and delivered a twenty-two-part sermon on conversion "as a public discourse… to an audience of scholars and students from the schools of Paris: Notre Dame, Saint Genevieve, and perhaps Saint Victor" (Evans 65). The religious foundation of these institutions notwithstanding, some of the listeners were presumably men of the world, yet Bernard acknowledges their probable familiarity with the Bible. He opens the first segment of his sermon with the words "You have come, I believe, to hear the Word of God," following this welcome with a reference to Acts of the Apostles 19:10: "All who lived in Asia came to hear the word of God, Jews and gentiles." Thus, Saint Bernard realizes that despite their scholarly occupations, the students and scholars know and can easily relate to these words from the Bible.

As we have seen in the foregoing examples, Catholics, both lay and clerical, were strongly encouraged to read the Bible, but the popes, Saint Jerome, and Gregory the Great all emphasize the importance of doing so under the guidance of teachers with qualifications endorsed by the Church, as opposed to each reader interpreting Scripture on his or her own. Using private judgment to interpret Scripture instead of following the magisterium of the Church is one of the major issues separating Catholics and Protestants. Fr. Forrest illustrates the inevitable confusion resulting from private judgment by comparing the Bible to a civil law. Suppose, he suggests, that each member of a given community were to interpret a law according to his or her own understanding and whim. Imagine the chaos that would ensue (77)! Plus, he explains, many biblical passages are obscure and must be read in their cultural and historical contexts: a background which most lay people do not possess. Finally, Father shows that the Bible itself forbids private, or individual, interpretation. As Saint Peter states, in the letters of Saint Paul, "[there] are certain things hard to understand, which the unlearned and unstable wrest, as they do other scriptures, to their own destruction" (2 Peter 3:16). Furthermore, chapter 8 in the Acts of the Apostles (27–35) also illustrates the folly of private judgment or individual interpretation. When Philip meets an Ethiopian reading Isaiah and asks if he comprehends what he is reading, the Ethiopian replies, "How can I unless someone shows me?"

Notes

1. This is not to say that the Church "comes from" the Bible. Obviously, the Old Testament existed long before the advent of Christianity, although, as the Reverend Henry G. Graham states, its many books were not all composed at the same time nor by the same writer. Graham goes on to explain that the books of the New Testament were not written until after Christ's resurrection, when the apostles were already celebrating the Mass and preaching the Word, and that "at least 40 years passed away between the writing of the first and the last of its books" (13). Moreover, the Church did not compile these books into one volume until the year 397, at the Council of Carthage. Prior to this time, many written accounts of the lives of Jesus and Mary circulated throughout Christendom, some more authentic than others. The purpose of the Council was to select the most authentic accounts and to regard the collection as the "correct, authoritative, reliable account…of Our Lord's life" (16). Therefore, the Church does not originate from the New Testament but precedes it by nearly four centuries.
2. According to the editor Gillian Evans, "the term 'conversion' at this date had, most commonly, the sense of 'deciding to enter a religious order,' but for Bernard it is also conversion of the heart" (65).

Works Cited

Bernard of Clairvaux. *Selected Works*. Edited and translated by Gillian R. Evans. New York: Paulist Press, 1987.

Council of Trent. *Canons and Decrees of the Council of Trent: Original Text with English Translation*. Edited and translated by the Reverend H. J. Schroeder, OP. Saint Louis: B. Herder Book Company, 1949.

Graham, Henry G. *Where We Got the Bible: Our Debt to the Catholic Church*. Aeterna Press, 2015.

Gregory the Great. *Pastoral Care (Regula Pastoralis)*. Edited by Johannes Quasten, STD, and Joseph Plump. Translated and annotated by Henry Davis, SJ. 1950. Reprint, New York: Newman Press, 1978.

Forrest, M. D., MSC. *Chats with Converts*. 1943. Reprint, Rockford, IL: Tan Books and Publishers Inc., 1978.

Hahn, Scott, and Kimberly Hahn. *Rome Sweet Home: Our Journey to Catholicism*. San Francisco: Ignatius Press, 1993.

Hatch, Alden, and Seamus Walshe. *Crown of Glory: The Life of Pope Pius XII*. New York: Hawthorn Books, Inc., 1958.

Holy Bible, Douay Rheims Version. Rockford, IL: Tan Books and Publishers Inc., 1971.

Jerome, Eusebius. "Letter 107: Ad Laetam." In *Sancti Eusebii Hieronymi Epistulae*, edited by Isidorus Hilberg, vol. 54. Vienna: Akademie Der Wissenschaften, 1996.

Ibid., "Letter 25: Ad Marcellam."

Ibid., "Letter 59: Ad Marcellam."

Ibid., "Letter 49: Ad Pammachium."

Ibid., "Letter 53: Ad Paulinum Presbyterum."

Ibid., "Letter 65: Ad Principiam."

Ibid., "Letter 11: Ad Virgines Haemonenses."

Pope Benedict XV. *Humani generis redemptionem.* Papal Encyclicals Online. Accessed October 24, 2017. http://www.papalencyclicals.net.

Pope Leo XIII. *Providentissimus Deus.* Ibid.

Pope Pius X. *Praestantia Scripturae.* Ibid.

Pope Pius XII. *Divino afflante Spiritu.* Ibid.

About the Author

Born in 1943, Rebecca Hinton grew up in Dayton, Ohio. She was married for fifty-one years to the late Huland Hinton, with whom she had five children. In 1990, Rebecca completed a doctorate in English from Miami University (Oxford, Ohio) and taught for more than twenty years at the University of Cincinnati as well as Saint Gertrude the Great High School (West Chester, Ohio). Now retired, she keeps busy by traveling, taking classes, and volunteering at a local animal shelter.